LOVE

A New Look at an Old Word

DON BAKER

HARVEST HOUSE PUBLISHERS
Eugene, Oregon 97402

LOVE

Copyright © 1988 by Harvest House Publishers
Eugene, Oregon 97402

Library of Congress Cataloging-in-Publication Data

Baker, Don.
  Love: a new look at an old word.

      1. Love—Biblical teaching.   2. Bible. N.T.
Corinthians, 1st, XIII—Criticism, interpretation, etc.
I. Title.
BS2655.L6B35 1988   241'.4   87-82260
ISBN 0-89081-642-5

Printed in the United States of America.

1 Corinthians 13

If I speak with the tongues of men and of angels, but do not have love, I have become a noisy gong or a clanging cymbal.

And if I have the gift of prophecy, and know all mysteries and all knowledge, and if I have all faith, so as to remove mountains, but do not have love, I am nothing.

And if I give all my possessions to feed the poor, and if I deliver my body to be burned, but do not have love, it profits me nothing.

Love is patient, love is kind, and is not jealous; love does not brag and is not arrogant,

Does not act unbecomingly; it does not seek its own, is not provoked, does not take into account a wrong suffered,

Does not rejoice in unrighteousness, but rejoices with the truth;

Bears all things, believes all things, hopes all things, endures all things.

Love never fails; but if there are gifts of prophecy, they will be done away; if there are tongues, they will cease; if there is knowledge, it will be done away.

For we know in part and we prophesy in part;

But when the perfect comes, the partial will be done away.

When I was a child, I used to speak as a child, think as a child, reason as a child; when I became a man, I did away with childish things.

For now we see in a mirror dimly, but then face to face; now I know in part, but then I shall know fully, just as I also have been fully known.

But now abide faith, hope, love—these three; but the greatest of these is love.

Contents

One

If I speak with the tongues of men and of angels, but do not have love, I have become a noisy gong or a clanging cymbal. And if I have the gift of prophecy, and know all mysteries and all knowledge, and if I have all faith, so as to remove mountains, but do not have love, I am nothing. And if I give all my possessions to feed the poor, and if I deliver my body to be burned, but do not have love, it profits me nothing.

1 Corinthians 13:1-3

1
What Is Love?

"Now's the time for you to prove your love for me," said the cult leader to his 968 followers as he led them in a mass suicide.

"I love you too much to let you suffer," said the 69-year-old husband to his dying wife as he placed a plastic bag over her head.

"We loved each other too much to wait," said the teenage couple faced with a premarital pregnancy.

"I love you too much to let you live," said the young mother as she dropped her newborn baby through the hole of an outdoor privy.

"I'm only doing this because I love you," said the angry father as he administered a fatal beating to his six-year-old child.

"But I love you," said the executive as he pled with his secretary to leave her family and marry him.

"I love you," said the father as he sexually molested his 15-year-old daughter.

We do some crazy things in the name of love, don't we?

Is it possible that the world still doesn't know what its favorite four-letter word really means?

In one of Charles Schulz's comic strips, Lucy says to Charlie Brown, "You know what I don't understand? I don't understand love."

Charlie Brown responds, "Who does?"

Lucy replied, "Explain love to me, Charlie Brown."

"I can't explain love. I can only recommend a book or a poem or a painting. I can't explain love," answers Charlie.

"Well, try, Charlie Brown, try."

Charlie says, "Well, let's say I see this beautiful, cute little girl walking by . . ."

Lucy interrupts, "Why does she have to be cute, huh? Explain that! Why can't someone fall in love with a person with freckles and a big nose? Explain that, Charlie Brown!"

"Well, maybe you're right," answers Charlie. "Let's just say I see this girl walk by with this *great* big nose . . ."

"I didn't say *great* big nose, Charlie."

In the last frame, his hands jammed down into his pockets, Charlie dejectedly walks away from Lucy and says, "You not only can't explain love, you can't even talk about it."

As I begin this book, I must confess that I am not an authority on the subject of love, nor do I mean to leave you with the impression that I am the world's greatest lover.

I am just another forgiven man whose love has been
    blunted by selfishness,

> dulled by ego,
>   obscured by anger,
>   smothered by ambition, and
>   extinguished by hate.

I was showing off a new Oldsmobile Cutlass to the family when our 12-year-old son wheeled into the driveway on his bicycle.

"Wow!" he said as he saw the car. He jumped off his bike and let it fall against the left front fender. I watched helplessly as the unprotected handlebar slid down the fender, scraping nearly 12 inches of shiny blue paint in the process.

John was horrified.

My wife was silent.

I was furious.

I picked up the bike, threw it into the garage, and railed at my son.

"Look at that!" I said, "Not even an hour old, and you've already ruined it! How can you be so careless, so stupid? You're going to have that fender repainted! I don't care how long it takes you to earn the money, you're going to pay to have that fixed!"

John shuffled off toward the house, his head bowed and his eyes filled with tears. As I watched him, my anger turned to shame.

I called him back and watched as his young body shook with fear. I lifted his chin until his eyes looked up into mine and said, "Son, do you have the feeling that I love this car more than I love you?"

He lowered his eyes, paused a long time, and then without a word nodded his head and began to cry.

"I guess it really looks that way, doesn't it?"

I placed my arm around him, attempted to reassure him of his importance to me, lamely apologized for my outburst, and then tried to recapture some of the excitement that was there before the accident.

It was gone.

All the joy of the moment was beyond reach. In its place was an ugly, lingering memory that still, 20 years later, refuses to die.

No, I'm not an authority on the subject of love. I am a man who still finds loving to be a problem.

The Christians at Corinth were struggling too. They had become so obsessed with their spiritual gifts that they had forgotten to control their carnal attitude.

Abilities were present and in use. Love was in short supply.

In his first letter to the Corinthians, Paul discussed their spiritual gifts. In chapters 12 and 14 their gifts are defined, described, and illustrated. He commends them for employing these gifts and then rebukes them for rating one gift above another.

Speaking in tongues was the rage in Corinth.

Right in the middle of his profound discussion he stops, places his sensitive finger on the erratic pulse of a carnal body of believers, and tells them that their ministry—whatever it might be—is worthless if their attitude is wrong.

He says:

If I speak with the tongues of men

and angels, but do not have love,
I have become a noisy gong or a
clanging cymbal (13:1).

"Tongues," no matter how exotic or com-
plex, without love are nothing more than noise
without meaning.

Even if I were able to master all of the 4000
languages or dialects of earth, or if I could super-
naturally communicate in
　　the 900 dialects of Asia,
　　　the 600 dialects of Europe,
　　　　the 300 dialects of Africa, or
　　　　　the 1100 dialects of the Americas,
　　　　or
if I could speak and pray in the languages of
heaven, and did so without love, it would all be
simply noise with meaning.

Gongs and cymbals are accompanying sounds.
They are not meant for solo use. When played
without the harmonic chords of love, they are
noise without meaning.

Paul continues,

If I have the gift of prophecy, and
know all mysteries and all knowledge, and if I have all faith, so as to
remove mountains, but do not have
love, I am nothing (13:2).

Prophecy was also an admired gift. It was
considered to be greater than others, but it too
was worthless without love.

If I possessed the rare gem of knowledge and could answer all the unanswerables of Scripture,

or

If I had sufficient faith to shift the mountains or move the hills from their places, but did not accompany those miracles with love, they would accomplish nothing more than startle the witnesses and change earth's geography.

> If I give all my possessions to feed the poor, and if I deliver my body to be burned, but do not have love, it profits me nothing (13:3).

Barnabas was quite a philanthropist. He sold his land and brought the money to be distributed among the poor (Acts 4:36,37).

He was commended, and the church was encouraged to follow his example.

Ananias and Sapphira sold their property and brought the money to the disciples for distribution among the poor. They were rebuked, they died, and the church was warned against a similar act.

The difference is to be found in the meaning of love. One act was profitable; the other was worthless.

Even if I hold up a lettered placard which reads "I Love Jesus" and then pour gasoline over my body and ignite it so that I'm burned to death, it's nothing but a waste of fuel, of life, and of time, unless it's done with love.

In just 89 words, the apostle Paul lays down a withering indictment on all of humanity. He tells us that the one ingredient that flavors all the relationships of life is love.

Without love, everything is tactless and repulsive.

Without love, our service is pointless and wasted.

Without love, life has no meaning.

Without love, ministry has no enduring quality.

Without love, I am nothing.

If love is that important to life and to eternity, then it's important that we understand what love is.

Two

*If I speak with the tongues of men and of angels,
but do not have love, I have become a noisy gong
or a clanging cymbal. And if I have the gift of
prophecy, and know all mysteries and all knowledge, and if I have all faith, so as to remove
mountains, but do not have love, I am nothing.
And if I give all my possessions to feed the poor,
and if I deliver my body to be burned, but do not
have love, it profits me nothing.*

1 Corinthians 13:1-3

2

Love Is from the Spirit

Most teaching on 1 Corinthians 13 is somewhat predictable.

Either I am going to be told to do
    something I am not doing, or to do
    something I cannot do, or to do
    something I don't want to do,
    or stop doing
      something I want to do.

At best, I am going to be told something I already know. That something I already know is that it's my responsibility to love.

I know that, but I can't do it—at least not like these verses suggest. The very first characteristic of love mentioned in verse 4 stops me cold. Patience is not natural to me. I am a terribly impatient person.

These 13 verses are not intended for a guilt trip or a journey up frustration alley. This chapter is not telling me how I should love; it's telling me how God loves.

Did you get that? This chapter is telling me how God loves.

These verses describe the genuine article.

These verses reveal God's love for mankind. It's a picture of love in clear and sharp focus.

The word for love here is *agape*. It's used eight times in these ten sentences.

Agape love is unique and incomparable.

Agape love is not common to man.

Since it has no counterpart in human experience, it's difficult to comprehend.

Since man does not have either the desire or the ability to duplicate agape love, it's impossible to copy.

Agape is the word the apostle John uses when he tells us that "God is love" (1 John 4:16) and when he reminds us that love originated in God (1 John 4:10).

Agape is the word Jesus used when He engaged Peter in that memorable dialogue by the Sea of Galilee after His resurrection (John 21:15-17).

Agape is the word that describes a love that is not human, not easy, and not popular.

Agape love has been defined as "unquenchable benevolence."

Unquenchable because it loves in spite of its responses.

Unquenchable because there is no limit to its duration.

Unquenchable because there is no end to its patience.

Unquenchable because it cannot be extinguished.

One can pour the icy waters of neglect or indifference or hatred over the burning flames of divine love as long as one wishes, but the love still cannot be quenched.

God's unquenchable love is

unending,
   undiminished,
      forever,
         eternal.

God's agape love is also benevolent.
Benevolent because it responds.
Benevolent because it acts.
Benevolent because it's demonstrable.
It's not a feeling, though it feels.
It's not an emotion, though it stirs.
It's *benevolent* because love is something God does.

In its benevolent form it has certain trademarks and leaves identifiable imprints on whatever it touches.

Again John refocuses the lens on love by stating:

> We know love by this, that He laid
> down His life for us; and we ought
> to lay down our lives for the breth-
> ren (1 John 3:16).

Love gives itself to others.

In its ultimate demonstration, it is God freely giving His only begotten Son as the sacrificial offering for all our sins.

In its mundane daily human demonstration, it is
      taking out the garbage,
         washing the dishes,
            ironing the handkerchiefs,
               providing for the family,

> earning a living,
> making the beds,
> cooking the meals,
> feeding the hungry, and
> clothing the poor.

Love is a visible act. It's something God does. It's something I do.

> It is not something I say.
> It is not something I feel.
> It is something I *do*.

> Whoever has the world's goods, and beholds his brother in need and closes his heart against him, how does the love of God abide in him? (1 John 3:17).

It is something that can be measured and weighed by its actions.

That's why this chapter is so important. It's here not to add to our feelings of guilt or frustration—it's here to help me distinguish between the true and the false, between the genuine and the counterfeit.

It's here to help me spot the impostor and to distinguish the deception.

It's here to keep people like us from doing stupid things in the name of love, like those people listed on the first page of the first chapter.

It's here not only to remind us of its importance, but also to remind us of our limitations—our imperfections.

It's here to constantly alert us to our need for love and our inability to demonstrate divine love without divine assistance.

It's here to remind us of our continuing dependence upon the Holy Spirit of God. He is the One who
    reveals agape love to us,
      places agape love within us,
        unfolds its mysteries for us, and then
          displays it through us.

For the "fruit of the Spirit is love" (Galatians 5:22).

Three

❦

Love is patient, love is kind, and is not jealous; love does not brag and is not arrogant.

1 Corinthians 13:4

3

Love Is Patient

Patience, or long-suffering, is an identifying mark of agape love.

Agape love accepts all that man can do to me without retaliation.

John Wesley was riding home late one night, singing one of his favorite hymns, when he was startled by a fierce voice shouting "Halt!" and a firm hand seizing his horse's bridle.

The man demanded, "Your money or your life!"

Wesley obediently emptied his pockets of the few coins they contained and invited the robber to examine his saddlebags, which were filled with books.

Satisfied that he had all that the preacher could give him, the robber started to walk away. Suddenly John Wesley cried, "Stop! I have something more to give you."

The startled robber turned back. Wesley bent down from his horse, handed the man his little Bible, and said, "My friend, you may live to regret this night. When you do, I plead with you to remember that . . . the blood of Jesus Christ, God's Son, cleanses us from all sin."

The robber hurried away, and the man of

God rode on toward home, praying that the Word of God might be fixed in the man's conscience.

Years later, at the close of a Sunday service, people streamed from the large building to speak with Mr. Wesley. A stranger stepped forward and begged to speak with Mr. Wesley. It was the robber, now a believer and a well-to-do businessman.

He took John Wesley's hand, put it to his lips, and said with deep emotion, "To you, sir, I owe it all."

"No, my friend," said Wesley, "not to me but to Jesus."

Agape love is patient; it does not seek its own revenge.

It does not create hostility or engender strife.

It returns love for hate, and by so doing it defuses all the weapons that our enemy has stockpiled against us.

In more recent years, the Mau Mau uprising in the African country of Kenya resulted in uncounted thousands of Christians being brutally mutilated and killed.

When Jomo Kenyatta and his Mau Mau followers were finally subdued, some were executed but thousands were sent to prison.

When an African is sent to prison for a long period of time, his family, left without support, often dies or is scattered.

The surviving remnant of the Christian church took in the families of its murderers. Wives, mothers, and children were housed, fed, clothed, and loved.

Upon release from prison years later, the former Mau Maus returned home, expecting to find their families dead or scattered. Instead, they found them intact, well-nourished, clothed, housed, and joyfully active in the Christian churches they had once tried to destroy.

That's agape love at work!

Love refuses to retaliate.

An act of vengeance is never an act of love.

Whenever I repay a hostile act with a hostile response, I am not demonstrating love.

A young woman, a stranger, was incensed when I casually greeted her in the church hallway with my very typical, "Hi, how are you?" greeting.

She stopped abruptly, then turned to me and said, "Don't you ever do that again! Don't you dare ask me how I am unless you're really concerned and want to know."

As the new pastor of a strange congregation, I was stunned.

I apologized, smoldered, and then tried to unravel this strange behavior. I finally decided that if this was going to be the response to my greetings, I would stop greeting people. I definitely decided against speaking to the woman whom I had offended.

My decision to not speak was not characteristic of agape love. My response to a hostile act was a very silent, but subtle, hostile response. I later repented of that decision, pursued her friendship, and won a friend in return.

Whatever the hostile act—whether it's physical harm or just plain old-fashioned "horn-cussing"

—whenever it is met with a hostile response, it is not a demonstration of love.

God's anger has a very long fuse. That controlled anger has resulted in some remarkable responses.

In Exodus chapter 16 we find the record of a disgruntled, complaining, miserable nation of freed slaves who were mad at Moses and at God for not providing them with enough food to eat while they walked from Egypt to Canaan.

How did God respond to this hostility?

He set up a catering service in heaven and then sent down a fresh supply of meat and bread daily.

That's the identifiable characteristic of agape love known as patience.

Just a few miles further, they did it again.

They complained because they were short of water. They even accused Moses of leading them to their deaths.

What did God do?

He opened a rock and caused pure water to flow from its depths.

That's love.

God is not vengeful.
God does not retaliate.
God does not harbor grudges.

The most strategic weapon that God employs against a hostile world is His infinite patience. It's a weapon against which there is no defense.

A hostile Roman, assisting in the crucifixion, was overcome when he heard Jesus say, "Father, forgive them."

That's love.

He responded by praising God and saying, "Certainly this man was innocent" (Luke 23:47).

That's the response to love.

The church of Jesus Christ today is weak, benign, and ineffective within its hostile communities because we are as hostile as they are.

The power of the church is diminished by the tasteless, childish infighting that persists. Our unnecessary little in-house wars make it virtually impossible to engage the real enemy in the greater conflict.

Pastors are being forced out of their churches and members are being scattered by all sorts of unnecessary controversy.

Only a few are willing to lose a battle in order to win a war.

A "love" that divides and criticizes and punishes is not agape love.

A "love" that cannot wait is not agape love.

A "love" that will not endure is not agape love.

A "love" that seeks its own revenge is not agape love.

A "love" that refuses to initiate reconciliation is not agape love.

A "love" that says it won't forgive is not agape love.

and

". . . if I do not have agape love, I am nothing."

The story is told of two mountain goats who approached each other on a narrow mountain ledge. Realizing there was no room to pass, they reared and bucked. Neither budged. They backed up and charged, then like large boulders stood unmovable.

Finally one knelt down and let the other climb over him. Both survived.

That's love, agape love, in its enduring, patient, long-suffering form.

Four

❦

Love is patient, love is kind, and is not jealous;
love does not brag and is not arrogant.

1 Corinthians 13:4

4

Love Is Kind

Kindness is an identifying mark of agape love.

Kindness seeks ways to improve another person's life.

Kindness looks for ways of being helpful.

Kindness rejects cruelty and looks for a way of being constructive.

I grew up in an era when liberals preached on love and conservatives preached on judgment.

Love was referred to as "sloppy agape."

There was very little open display of affection. We seldom held hands with fellow believers.

We never hugged.

The words "I love you" were reserved for only one person, and even then they were rarely used.

During my siege in the black hole of depression, I withdrew from my family and from my church.

On one of those self-imposed exiles in Santa Barbara, California, I was completely disarmed and conquered by a simple, unobtrusive act of love's kindness.

It was in the days of the flower children, the hippies, and the love-ins.

I was offended by the "dropouts" from civilization and resented their communal living and drug dependence and hairstyles. They were repulsive to me.

One night I was feeling very lonely and decided to go for a walk. As I passed the open door of a deserted store, I heard the faint sounds of a guitar and singing. I walked back to the door and looked in.

There, about a hundred young people dressed in their typical garb, were singing praise hymns that were filled with expressions of love for God. A young barefoot man dressed in cutoffs and a tank top was leading them with his guitar.

I was irresistibly drawn to that large room crowded with wall-to-wall people.

I sat down on the floor like the others, but just outside the door. I didn't want to be seen. I didn't want to be a part of whatever was happening, but I did want to observe.

A young man stood to teach. He had a dog-eared little New Testament in his hand, a warm and infectious smile, and a disarming manner. I found myself listening in spite of myself.

He announced his text. Since I didn't have my Bible with me, I was unable to follow along as he read. As he was reading, I became aware of another young man watching me. He would read for a few seconds and then look over at me. He would then lower his eyes back to the page again. Finally he got up from his place on the floor, moved toward me, and sat down beside me.

He didn't know me. The only things he had noticed were that I was obviously over 30, differently dressed, and alone—and that I didn't have a Bible.

His hair was greasy, long, and shaggy.
He wore no shirt.
His cutoffs were dirty.
He wore beads on his head
and around his neck.
His feet were bare and filthy.
He looked over into my clouded eyes, smiled, and said "Hi."

He shoved his little New Testament in front of me and whispered, "This is a Bible. We're reading from page 96." He then pointed his long, dirty fingernail at the right verse and said, "Would you like to read it with me?"

He held it up in front of my face and traced the words with his finger.

I couldn't see a thing. My eyes filled with tears. Those tears blurred my glasses and spilled down over my cheeks. I began to sob so uncontrollably that I got to my feet and hurried out into the night.

I was conquered by kindness.

Agape love is kind. It looks for ways of meeting the needs of others.

For 38 years I have watched people as they file into church services. From my vantage point on the platform I see things that others seldom see.

It's always disturbing to watch the low level of kindness displayed by many Christians.

Latecomers will be forced to climb over the feet of the comfortable who refuse to move.

Some will be unable to find a hymnbook and others unable to locate the page. Only a few will offer to help. Most people never even notice.

Some will scowl as they're asked to move their coats; others will be angered if they find their favorite seat occupied.

Agape love is kind.

It seeks for ways of being helpful.

God is kind. It's His nature to be kind.

God's kindness is displayed in
   the sun that warms us,
      the clouds that shade us,
         the rain that cools us,
            the moon that lightens
            our darkness, and
               the flowers that give
                  beauty to our world.

God's kindness is not conditional; it is displayed in spite of our sinfulness.

In Romans chapter 1 Paul describes unrighteousness. He uses words like
   idolatrous,
      immoral,
         unnatural,
            depraved,
               corrupt, and without any redeeming qualities of any kind.

In Romans chapter 2 Paul describes self-righteousness. It is just as offensive to God. He refers to the judgment that is leveled against hypocrisy, and then questions man's indifference to God's infinite kindness which restrains Him from sending judgment upon both the unrighteous and the self-righteous.

God's kindness provides for man's needs even when man is unaware of them.

God's kindness provides for man's needs even when man won't admit to having them.

God's kindness provides for man's needs even in response to man's cruelty.

Agape love is kind.

I often eat my noon meals at McDonald's. My favorite is a Quarter Pounder with Cheese and a small diet Coke. I'm often in a hurry and usually distracted, so I like my fast-food restaurant to provide my food as fast as possible.

I drove to my nearby McDonald's recently, pulled up to the speaker, and waited. Soon I heard the familiar,

"Welcome to McDonald's. May I take your order, please?"

"Yes, I'd like a Quarter Pounder with Cheese and a small diet Coke."

"Would you like an order of French fries with that, sir?"

"No, thank you."

"That will be $3.72, sir."

"How much?"

"$3.72, sir."

"No, that's $2.16, ma'am. I ordered a Quarter Pounder with Cheese and a small diet Coke."

"You ordered *two* Quarter Pounders with Cheese and a diet Coke, *sir*."

"No, *ma'am*, I ordered *one* Quarter Pounder with Cheese."

"That will be $2.16, *sir*." Click—end of conversation.

I was "ticked." That's a much less threatening way of saying I was angry. Why didn't she acknowledge her mistake? Why didn't she at least say something like, "Oh, I'm sorry, sir."

Then I got to thinking. In less than two minutes I'm going to look that lady right in the eyeballs. She's going to ask for my $2.16, and I'm going to give it to her. What am I going to say?

I could continue the argument.

I could rebuke her for not apologizing.

I could insult her by saying something like, "You ought to turn up your hearing aid."

I could give a very cold and heartless "Thank you."

I could do worse and just say nothing.

or

I could be kind and say, "I'm sorry, I'll try to speak more clearly next time."

What would you do?

Well, this time I did the right thing. I was kind, and it made the day a little brighter for both of us.

Agape love is kind. It looks for ways of being constructive.

Jesus was terribly distracted as He climbed the stairs to an upper room to eat with His disciples. He was about to die. He knew when, He knew where, and He knew how.

It's terribly difficult to think of meeting another person's needs when your own are that great.

As He entered the room, He noticed that a grave social error had just been committed. No one had thought to offer to wash the dusty feet of the 13 men who had just arrived.

Jesus rose up from the table, laid aside His garments, poured water into a basin, and began to wash the disciples' feet. He then wiped them with the towel that was wrapped around His waist.

Agape love is kind.

I'll never forget the Sunday, after a particularly busy and stressful week, that I returned home from church to find that my neighbor had mowed my lawn for me.

Agape love is kind.

It looks for constructive ways to meet the needs of others.

Five

❧

Love is patient, love is kind, and is not jealous;
love does not brag and is not arrogant.

1 Corinthians 13:4

5

Love Is Not Jealous

Freedom is an identifying mark of agape love.

Agape love is not possessive.

It does not hold exclusive, restrictive control over another person.

It allows for room to breathe, space to grow, and freedom to experience fulfillment.

Jealousy says, "I want you for myself," and then proceeds to restrict and confine and limit so that no other choices are available.

Love does not seek to control. It does not smother.

A dear friend was the victim of his mother's jealousy.

He was a godly man, a deacon, and a hard worker—who lived with his mother. He was completely dominated by her.

At age 55 he had never dated, had never been away from home overnight, and had never made any significant decision without his mother's input.

His mother had always encouraged him to date and to marry, but whenever he suggested the name of a woman to her, she immediately expressed disapproval.

I remember his bewilderment when at 86 years old his mother died. He was like a lost child. He called me and asked if I thought it would be all right if he took a woman to dinner.

Agape love is not jealous.

We parents are often guilty of holding the reins to our children too tightly. It's hard to let go. When the children are small, we tell them the difference between right and wrong, and we should. But often when they start forming opinions of their own and arrive at conclusions different from ours, we react with mild astonishment, even furious indignation.

We cannot possess their minds. If we could, we would create monsters, or worse, people like ourselves.

Love is not possessive.

It allows room to grow.

It permits opportunities to make mistakes.

Only God has the right to be possessive, but even He relinquishes the right.

In Genesis 2:7 we are told that

> . . . the Lord God formed man of dust from the ground, and breathed into his nostrils the breath of life; and man became a living being.

In Genesis 2:21,22 that same God

> . . . caused a deep sleep to fall upon the man, and he slept; then He took one of his ribs, and closed up the flesh at that place. And the Lord God fashioned into a woman the rib

which He had taken from the man,
and brought her to the man.

God made man, then God made woman.

Adam and Eve were God's creation. They were His. He had the unique right to possess them, to own them. He could have restricted their freedom, directed their movements, controlled their thoughts.

God chose to not possess them. He gave them room and permitted them opportunity to choose. He even gave them the liberty to sin.

In permitting them the liberty to sin, He gave them the right to choose another God above Himself. They chose another God.

Love is not jealous.

A young wife confessed to me that she had committed adultery. Her shame consumed her. She cried uncontrollably as she told me her story.

When she was finished, she lifted her head from her hands and asked,

"Why did God allow me to do it?

"Why didn't He stop me?

"Oh, how I wish He had stopped me.

"I begged Him to, but He didn't."

He could have stopped Adam and Eve too, but He didn't. It's the risk that love takes when it refuses to control. God wants our love to be free, uncontrolled, and willing. He wants our love to be genuine.

Every pastor understands the problem of the parishioner who wants to own him. It's always some sort of a crazy compliment, but it always causes some sort of crazy problem.

Some try it with money, others with gifts. It's usually some sort of unrestrained friendliness that is difficult to resist.

It reality, it is jealousy—a desire to control, the will to possess.

In the story of the prodigal son, we are introduced to a most remarkable father. He was willing to give his son his inheritance before he was legally eligible for it and long before he was physically capable of handling it.

The son wasted it, as his father knew he would.

> He wound up penniless and ashamed,
>   as his father had expected.
>   He returned home, as his father
>   had hoped.
>   He asked his father's forgiveness,
>   as the father had prayed, and
>   He was restored, as the father
>   had dreamed.

That was some father.

That was some love.

He allowed his son the mistakes that were necessary to grow up.

He permitted himself the pain of loss in order to later experience the joy of love.

Agape love is not jealous.

It's willing to let go. It refuses to control or possess.

Six

Love is patient, love is kind, and is not jealous;
love does not brag and is not arrogant.

1 Corinthians 13:4

6

Love Does Not Boast

Humility is an identifying mark of agape love.

Agape love does not boast.

It does not parade itself.

It does not seek to make an impression or create an image for personal gain.

As a child I memorized 1 Corinthians 13 and recited it many times.

I learned it in the King James Version.

The word "charity" was used in place of the word "love." That confused me. The two words were not synonymous in my thinking.

"Charity" was something I did for the poor. "Love" was something I felt.

Another word that was even more confusing was the word "vaunteth."

No matter how many times I recited verse 4, I never stopped to learn what the word "vaunteth" meant.

"Vaunteth" is a good word. It's just different enough to be memorable.

Vaunting is something we all do but shouldn't.

We all have this insatiable need to make others think well of us.

We must impress.

We boast, we brag, we find all sorts of subtle ways to exalt other people's opinions of us.

"Love vaunteth not itself."

I heard the story of a new lawyer in his new office on the first day of his new practice.

A prospective client walked through the door.

The young lawyer felt the need to "vaunt" a little. He immediately busied himself, picked up his phone, and started talking.

"Look, Harry," he said. "About that amalgamation deal, I think I'd better run down to the factory and handle it myself. Yes. No. I don't think a million will swing it. We'd better have Rogers from Seattle handle it. Okay. Call you back later."

The young lawyer laid down the phone, looked up at his visitor, and said, "Good morning. How may I help you?"

The prospective client said, "You can't help me at all. I'm from the phone company. I'm here to hook up your new telephone."

Love does not seek to impress.

When I was in the fifth grade, I had a close friend with whom I did daily battle.

Every afternoon on our way home from school we would pass a vacant lot that had a high sand hill. We would put down our lunch pails, pull off our sweaters, and proceed to play "King of the Mountain."

The idea of the game was to see who could get to the top first and stay there the longest.

We would scramble on our hands and knees through that soft sand until we reached the peak.

We would each grab the other and try to throw him down.

No one ever won. We just changed positions. I would be on top for awhile and then my friend would tackle me and throw me over the side. I would roll to the bottom, get up, spit sand out of my mouth, push the hair out of my eyes, and start back up again.

On one occasion I had thrown my friend down and was king for awhile. I threw my head back, beat my chest, and let out that old familiar Tarzan yell. I shouted it long and loud.

That was vaunting. I was drawing everyone's attention to my achievement. I was obviously trying to impress.

That was a kid's way of saying,

"I'm at the top of the heap."
"King of the road."
"Ruler of this mountain."

We have far more sophisticated ways of "vaunting" today. We seldom slap our chests and deliver an African yodel.

We make our statements in others ways— with our cars, our houses, our clothes, and even our friends. We are obsessed with the need to let others know how great we are.

Love doesn't do that.

When I was in high school, no student owned his own car but me. It was a 1928 Chevy coupe with a rumble seat. It had four headlights and 26 taillights. The dashboard was finished in Chinese red.

I had bought it for 40 dollars, but the statement it made each morning as I drove into the school parking lot was worth millions to me.

Love doesn't do that.

Love uses a car for transportation, not to impress people.

The disease of the inflated ego was in the early church, especially in Corinth. They were constantly engaged in power plays, with each person struggling to be king of the mountain—top of the heap. The party spirit was rampant, with each person jockeying for a position of prominence or power by claiming that his spiritual gift was superior or that he was a convert of Paul, or Apollos, or Peter, or even Christ.

The same disease is in the church today.

It's in me.

Preachers are not supposed to be vain or proud. We're not supposed to brag or "vaunt"—but we do.

We have unbridled ambitions.

We have carnal goals.

We like to make statements that cover us with vainglory.

We like to wrap ourselves in our own "Shekinah" and impress people.

Even pastors are looking for
  larger churches,
    bigger buildings,
      higher salaries,
        finer cars,
          better houses, and
            costlier clothes.

We seek out the places of greatest political prominence, just like everybody else. I'm not proud of that.

The ultimate, unexpressed goal of most pastors used to be the conferral of the honorary doctor of divinity degree. It was the sought-after prize.

I will always remember that very dignified but happy service when that honorary degree was conferred upon me.

The commencement service was conducted in my own church. My mother was in the balcony. My wife was on the platform with the faculty. My children were seated in the audience.

I delivered the commencement address.

Dr. Earl Radmacher conferred the degree upon me. He read a lengthy letter of commendation that listed all the "wonderful" things I had ever done and even some "wonderful" things I hadn't done.

As profoundly moving as the ceremony was, all of its memories were obscured by the fact that I couldn't remember what side of the cap the tassel was supposed to go on.

Oh, how good it sounded to hear the words "Doctor Baker"!

Occasionally, when I'm feeling inferior, I'll use it. Often when I'm in a hurry, I use it. For some reason it seems that I get much better service.

When our daughter, Kathryn, was in the hospital in Portland for the birth of her first child, I called long-distance from Rockford.

Patient Information answered the phone. "This is Doctor Baker, calling from Rockford, Illinois. Will you connect me with Maternity, please?"

"Certainly, doctor. Right away."

Maternity answered and again I said, "This is Doctor Baker calling. I'd like to check on the progress of Mrs. Kathryn Barram, please."

"Just a moment, doctor."

The voice came back quickly and said, "Let me connect you with the fourth-floor nursing station."

Fourth-floor answered and again I said, "This is Doctor Baker calling from Rockford, Illinois. Would you give me a progress report on Kathryn Barram, please."

"Just a moment, please, doctor, I'll get her nurse."

Her nurse answered. I said it again: "This is Doctor Baker calling from Rockford, Illinois. I'd like to check on Kathryn Barram, please."

There was a pause. The voice from the hospital said, "Doctor Baker? Doctor Baker? Oh, Pastor Baker. I'm Kathy's nurse. We went to school together. Let me connect you with her room."

That was vaunting and that was embarrassing.

I would have been much better off if I had just said, "This is Kathy's daddy. How's my daughter doing?"

Love doesn't seek to impress for the sake of personal gain.

In Philippians chapter 2, agape love is beautifully modeled by Jesus. It's the account of the self-humbling of Jesus as He voluntarily stepped down from His position of glory to His place of shame.

In verses 5 to 8 He is described as stepping down
to earth,
to manhood,
to slavery,
to crucifixion, and
to death.

Most of us want to step up.
Jesus stepped down.

He let go of
His divine glory,
His heavenly environment,
His incalculable wealth, and
The independent exercise
of His attributes.
And He did all of this willingly.

Love refuses to lift itself up.
Love refuses to exalt itself or to seek to make an impression.
Love is willing to let go.
A Chinese Christian dreamed he was in a deep hole—a hole too deep for escape.
In his dream, Confucius walked to the edge of the hole, leaned over the edge, and offered his advice.
"Wise man never falls in hole," he said.
Buddha came by, leaned over the edge, and said, "Climb halfway up and I will bring you the rest of the way."

Jesus came by, leaned over the edge, looked down, saw the helpless condition of the man, and then dropped to the bottom in order to save the man from death.

That's love.

Love lowers itself.

Love doesn't lift itself up.

Agape love does not boast, brag, or seek to impress others for personal gain.

Love does not "vaunt."

Seven

Love does not act unbecomingly; it does not seek its own, is not provoked, does not take into account a wrong suffered.

1 Corinthians 13:5

7

Love Is Courteous

Decency is an identifying mark of agape love.
Agape love does not act out of character.
It never perverts itself in any way.
It always acts in the best interest of others.

The name of Linda Lovelace is not a household name among Christians. It is probably not too well known among the young. But in the 1970's Hugh Hefner called her the new sex goddess of America.

She replaced the Betty Grables and the Marilyn Monroes and the Elizabeth Taylors of filmdom. She took suggestive sex out of its wrappings and became the queen of the pornographic movie industry.

A few years ago she starred in a film called "Deep Throat." The picture took only 12 days to produce and has been seen around the world. It has netted its producers hundreds of millions of dollars and has been acclaimed as the greatest sex film ever made.

It was pure (or rather impure) porn—X-rated porn and as degrading and dirty as a film could be.

Those who viewed the film didn't see the real action. That took place backstage. It involved pistol whippings and beatings and kickings administered by two men, Chuck Trayner and Chuck Winters, whenever Linda Lovelace, the star, refused to do the dirty things they demanded of her.

She refers to her appearance in "Deep Throat" as a public rape, forcibly imposed upon her in front of cameras for the whole world to see.

On the cover of her book, entitled *Ordeal*, is the picture of a little red ceramic heart that is split from top to bottom—broken and beyond repair.

On the first page of the first chapter of her second book she says:

> I haven't been able to escape Linda Lovelace, but I have been able to make peace with her. I understand her and I understand what happened to her. My particular concern is for my 3½-year-old son. He will someday learn that his mother was once this woman named Linda Lovelace. He will surely hear one side of the story—the side that comes with a sneer and dirty laughter. I want him to hear it all.

She tells about her new life in Jesus Christ and how she is now vainly trying to forget a sordid past that will haunt her as long as she lives.

Love wouldn't allow a thing like that.

Agape love would not exploit a woman, or a man, for personal gain.

Agape love does not act indecently.

Agape love never acts irresponsibly.

It never perverts itself in any way.

Agape love wouldn't have exploited a Linda Lovelace and produced a pornographic film for the world to see.

Agape love wouldn't have watched the film, either.

Love wouldn't have done a thing like that.

The book of Romans, chapter 1, verses 24-27, deals with another perversion of love. It refers to homosexuality and describes it as

an unseemly act
   of degraded passions and
      unnatural functions.

It describes men and women burning in their desires for one another and performing their indecent acts.

Love wouldn't do a thing like that.

Love does not act unbecomingly.

Jerry was a practicing homosexual. I told his true story in the book entitled *Beyond Rejection*.

For 21 years he lived in his own little private hell.

He stopped long enough to get married, but then just 91 days after his wedding he went back to frequenting the gay bars of his hometown.

He has now been delivered.

He is helping others to break free from the power of homosexuality. He is now the one telling others, "Love wouldn't do a thing like that."

Love does not act unbecomingly.

In 1 Corinthians chapter 6 Paul says,

Flee immorality. Every other sin that a man commits is outside the

> body, but the immoral man sins against his own body.

> Do you not know that the one who joins himself to a harlot is one body with her?

Love wouldn't do a thing like that.

In 1 Corinthians chapter 7 Paul says,

> A wife should not leave her husband and a husband should not leave his wife.

Love wouldn't do a thing like that.

In the same chapter he says that a wife would not deprive her husband of the sexual fulfillment he needs, or that a husband would not deprive his wife of the sexual fulfillment she needs.

Love wouldn't do a thing like that.

I have walked through the pain and disbelief of fellow Christians who have been snagged by temptation and destroyed by sin.

I have sat with the young mother who dreams of the babies she has thrown away through abortion and prays for a baby that she is no longer able to have.

Love doesn't do things like that.

David the psalmist said,

> I will set no impure thing before my eyes.

If all of us were to make the same vow, the pornographic industry would go broke and all the sensual trash on television would have no viewers because love just does not cater to a crowd that generates its support by arousing the sensual appetites of their audiences.

Love wouldn't do a thing like that.

Love does not act unbecomingly.

Perverse and immoral acts are not the only things love does not do.

The word "unbecoming" is also used to describe unresolved differences or factious divisions within the church.

In 1 Corinthians 11:18,19 we are told that Christians are not to gather at the communion table as long as conflicts among members are not reconciled.

Love wouldn't do a thing like that, either.

The word "unbecomingly" refers to anything and everything from discourtesy to indecency.

A love that is becoming is
  courteous and
    kind and
      sensitive and
        caring.

It looks for hurts in others and then ministers to them until they're healed.

A love that is becoming feels pain and shares it. It never inflicts it.

It senses need and ministers to it.

It may offer nothing more than a smile or a touch. Whatever it offers, it is enough to let another person know that you heard and that you care.

Love does not exploit.

Love does not pervert.

Love does not ignore.

Agape love cares and responds.

Five-year-old Mary underwent an operation and lost so much blood that it was necessary to resort to a blood transfusion. Samples of blood of all the adult members of the family were taken, but none was found to match Mary's. A test was taken of her older brother's blood. It was a match. Jimmy, a husky boy of 13, cared deeply for his little sister.

"Will you give your sister some of your blood, Jim?" asked the doctor.

Jimmy set his teeth and said, "Yes, sir, if she needs it."

The need was desperate. The boy was prepared for the transfusion. In the midst of the blood transfer, the doctor noticed that Jimmy was growing quite pale.

"Are you feeling sick, Jim?" asked the doctor.

"No, sir, but I'm wondering just when I'll die."

"Die?" gasped the doctor. "Do you think people die when they give a little blood?"

"Yes, sir," replied Jimmy.

"And you were willing to die for your sister?"

"Yes, sir," replied the boy.

That's what love does.

Love gives. It doesn't take.

Love never acts out of character.

Love is not rude, or crude, or lewd.

Agape love does not act unbecomingly.

Agape love always acts in the best interests of others.

Eight

Love does not act unbecomingly; it does not seek its own, is not provoked, does not take into account a wrong suffered.

1 Corinthians 13:5

8

Love Is Unselfish

Unselfishness is an identifying mark of agape love.

Agape love does not pursue selfish advantage.

It does not demand its own way.

This costs, but love is willing to pay the price.

Dr. A. J. Gordon, a pastor in Boston for many years, saw a little boy in front of his church building. The boy was carrying a rusty bird cage. Several little birds were fluttering in the cage as if they knew they were about to be destroyed.

Dr. Gordon said, "Son, where did you get those birds?"

"I trapped them in the field."

"What are you going to do with them?" the preacher asked.

"I'm going to take them home and have some fun with them."

"What will you do with them when you get through playing with them?"

"Oh," said the boy, "I guess I'll just feed them to an old cat we have around the house."

"How much will you take for those birds?" Dr. Gordon asked.

"Mister, you don't want these birds. They're

just little old field birds, and they can't even sing very well."

"I'll give you two dollars for the cage and the birds," said Dr. Gordon.

The boy's eyes lit up, and he said, "All right, it's a deal. But you're making a bad bargain."

The exchange was made, and the boy went whistling down the street.

The Boston pastor then took the battered old cage with its fluttering prisoners out behind the church building. He opened the cage door and released them. The worthless little field birds went soaring away into the sky, singing as they went.

The next Sunday Dr. Gordon took the empty bird cage into his pulpit and used it to illustrate his sermon.

"The little boy said that the birds couldn't sing very well," he said. "Yet when I released them from their cage, they went singing away into the blue, and it seems that they were singing,

> Redeemed, how I love to proclaim
> it—
> Redeemed by the blood of the lamb!
> Redeemed by His infinite mercy,
> His child and forever I am.

Dr. Gordon's simple act of purchasing and freeing a cage filled with helpless field birds teaches something very profound about love. It teaches us that love,

> agape love,
> 1 Corinthians 13 type of love
> is expensive.

Agape love costs something to share with others.

Agape love does not seek its own.

It does not pursue selfish advantage.

It does not demand its own way.

It is not selfish.

A young wife had been praying that her husband would receive Christ. When it happened, he didn't tell her.

"But I knew," she said. "I knew that God had gotten hold of him and had changed him."

"How did you know?" asked her friend.

"He took out the garbage," she replied excitedly.

"Took out the garbage?" her friend asked.

"Yes, he took out the garbage. Since we've been married I have never been able to get him to take out the garbage. But now for three nights in a row he has taken out the garbage, and I haven't even had to ask him."

Love does not seek its own.

Love desires to meet the needs of others.

The ultimate example of unselfish love is found in Galatians 4:4-6:

> When the fulness of time came, God sent forth His Son, born of a woman, born under the Law, in order that He might redeem those who were under the Law, that we might receive the adoption as sons. And because you are sons, God has sent forth the Spirit of His Son into our hearts, crying, "Abba! Father!"

Those verses point us to the New Testament picture of redemption: the freeing of captives and then enabling them to sing a song never heard while in captivity.

But notice—it cost something.

"In the fulness of time . . ." At just the right moment. At least 4000 years after sin entered the world and took its inhabitants captive—

After the whole story had been told in advance

After the prophecy had been completed

After the Scriptures had been made available

After Greece and then Rome had united the civilized world

After earth had learned to speak one common language

After Roman roads had made all the nations of the earth accessible

After the Jews had been dispersed

And while the world was at peace

And in a moment of time when Mary wasn't distracted

And the shepherds were listening

And wise men were expectant.

In that precise moment of time, when the world was convinced that it was helplessly imprisoned in the cage of its own sin,

"God sent forth His Son."

This, in just five words of one syllable each, is the high cost of loving, in clear focus and on display for all to see.

This is love made visible, demonstrable, see-able.

This is love resisting its own desires and giving

away something of infinite value because there is a need.

That illustration of love's unselfishness points to a unique Father-Son relationship at a point of extreme crisis—a Father and Son about to experience separation.

"God sent forth His Son."

There is something very special about a father-son relationship.

Every father desires a son. That's not to the discredit of a daughter. Not at all. Father-son relationships are different—not better, but different.

Fathers want sons to carry on their name and, if possible, their careers.

A father sees in his son a chance to start over again and to possibly do better.

God has a Son.

God the Father has a Son. We are often so consumed with the differences in God's relationship to His Son that we overlook the obvious similarities.

The mysteries of trinity and deity sometimes obscure the wonders of humanity.

It is true that God's relationship to His Son is different.

It is different in that God the Father was never older than His Son.

God the Father was never smarter than His Son.

God the Father was never stronger than His Son.

God the Father was never wiser than His Son.

God the Father never rocked His Son in a cradle.

He never sent Him off to kindergarten.

He never encouraged Him in big-muscle development.

He never played ball with Him.

God's relationship to His Son is different.

For God the Father and God the Son are co-eternal.

They have both existed forever, neither one superior to the other, until—God sent forth His Son.

It was then that something changed.

It was then that God the Son became willingly submissive to God the Father.

It was then that Jesus left home.

It was then that His heavenly space was vacated.

It was then that His room was left empty.

It was then that the Father said "Goodbye" to His Son.

Has it ever occurred to you that it was painful to God when Jesus left home?

Several years ago we sent our son to his first pastorate. When that day finally ended, I sat in the quietness of the late evening and put my feelings down on a piece of paper.

"My son left home today," I said. As I watched him walk through the door tall and erect, climb into his car, and drive down the winding street, I knew that this time it was for good. I watched him until he was out of sight and then I slowly drove back to the office.

Tears made driving difficult. The rush of years of memories made concentration impossible.

That evening I walked aimlessly through the house, studying the empty space where years of accumulated memories had been stored.

There was the collection of Matchbox cars that even his dad played with occasionally.

Three baseball gloves and baseball shoes were among the missing items. The backpack, sleeping bag, Ping-Pong table, tennis balls, golf clubs, skis—all were gone. All those things that had appeared as clutter now took on great value, but all were gone.

The books, hundreds of them, were missing.

The piano was silent.

Door keys, often misplaced, jangled noisily in my pocket. The driveway, previously cluttered with cars, now allowed me all the parking space I needed.

Little drops of engine oil on concrete—at one time a point of serious contention—but now I wouldn't wipe them up for all the world.

His room was cold and silent.

His closet was bare.

His dog was bewildered and listless.

His parents were both full and empty.

Neither of us dared speak. Finally, unable to stand it any longer, we fell into each other's arms, weeping that strange combination of tears of joy and tears of sadness.

When God's Son left home, there must have been the pain of emptiness—of loneliness.

And yet, there was a greater pain.

God's Son was also leaving to become a pastor, not of a warm, caring congregation but of a cold, hostile world—an unbelieving, arrogant, sin-cursed world that would eventually turn against Him and destroy Him.

When God the Father sent His Son, He saw the stable and the manger.

He saw the star, and He watched the shepherds.

He heard the angels and looked at the wise men.

He also saw a hostile king prepared to kill Him.

He saw crowds anxious to destroy Him.

He saw the religious reject Him and the temple expel Him.

He saw angry crowds and a cruel cross.

He saw thorns and spikes and a spear.

He saw Calvary in bold relief.

He looked down and saw that inevitable moment when He would be forced to ignore the cries of His only Son.

God the Father saw it all in advance and knew all that would happen, but He still sent forth His Son.

God saw it all. He sent Him anyway.

That's love.

Love seeks not its own.

Love lets go.

Love is not selfish.

Agape love costs, but it's willing to pay the price.

Nine

❧

Love does not act unbecomingly; it does not seek its own, is not provoked, does not take into account a wrong suffered.

1 Corinthians 13:5